SHARK
PICTURES
SHARK BOOKS FOR KIDS

Speedy Publishing LLC
40 E. Main St. #1156
Newark, DE 19711

www.SpeedyPublishing.Com

Copyright 2014
978-1-63287-409-2
First Printed May 30, 2014

 speedypublishing

There are more than 465 known species of sharks living in our oceans today.

Sharks are an apex predator at or near the top of their marine food chains, and they regulate the populations of species below them.

Research has shown that massive depletion of sharks has cascading effects throughout the ocean's ecosystems.

Sharks belong to a family of fish that have skeletons made of cartilage, a tissue more flexible and lighter than bone.

Sharks breathe through a series of five to seven gill slits located on either side of their bodies.

All sharks have multiple rows of teeth, and while they lose teeth on a regular basis, new teeth continue to grow in and replace those they lose.

Scientists can determine the age of a shark by counting the rings that form on its vertebra, much as you can count the rings on a tree to tell its age.

The upper side of a shark is generally dark to blend in with the water from above and their undersides are white or lighter colored to blend in with the lighter surface of the sea from below.

Most species of shark eat things like fish, crustaceans, mollusks, plankton, krill, marine mammals and other sharks.

Sharks have adapted to living in a wide range of aquatic habitats at various temperatures. While some species inhabit shallow, coastal regions, others live in deep waters, on the ocean floor and in the open ocean.

Most sharks are especially active in the evening and night when they hunt. Some sharks migrate over great distances to feed and breed.

While some shark species are solitary, others display social behavior at various levels. Hammerhead sharks, for instance, school during mating season around seamounts and islands.

Some shark species, like the great white shark, attack and surprise their prey, usually seals and sea lions, from below.

Species that dwell on the ocean floor have developed the ability to bottom-feed. Others attack schooling fish in a feeding frenzy, while large sharks like the whale and basking sharks filter feed by swimming through the ocean with their mouths open wide, filtering large quantities of plankton and krill.

Sharks do not have a single bone in their bodies. Instead they have a skeleton made up of cartilage; the same type of tough, flexible tissue that makes up human ears and noses.

Sharks have outstanding hearing. They can hear a fish thrashing in the water from as far as 500 metres away!

A pup (baby shark) is born ready to take care of itself. The mother shark leaves the pup to fend for itself and the pup usually makes a fast get away before the mother tries to eat it.

Not all species of shark give birth to live pups. Some species lay the egg case on the ocean floor and the pup hatches later on its own.

If a shark was put into a large swimming pool, it would be able to smell a single drop of blood in the water.

A shark always has a row of smaller teeth developing behind its front teeth. Eventually the smaller teeth move forward, like a conveyor belt, and the front teeth fall out.

Great whites are the deadliest shark in the ocean. These powerful predators can race through the water at 30 km per hour.

Although most species of shark are less than one metre long, there are some species such as the whale shark, which can be 14 metres long.

The chance of being killed by a shark is one in 300 million. The chance of being killed by airplane parts falling from the sky is one in 10 million.

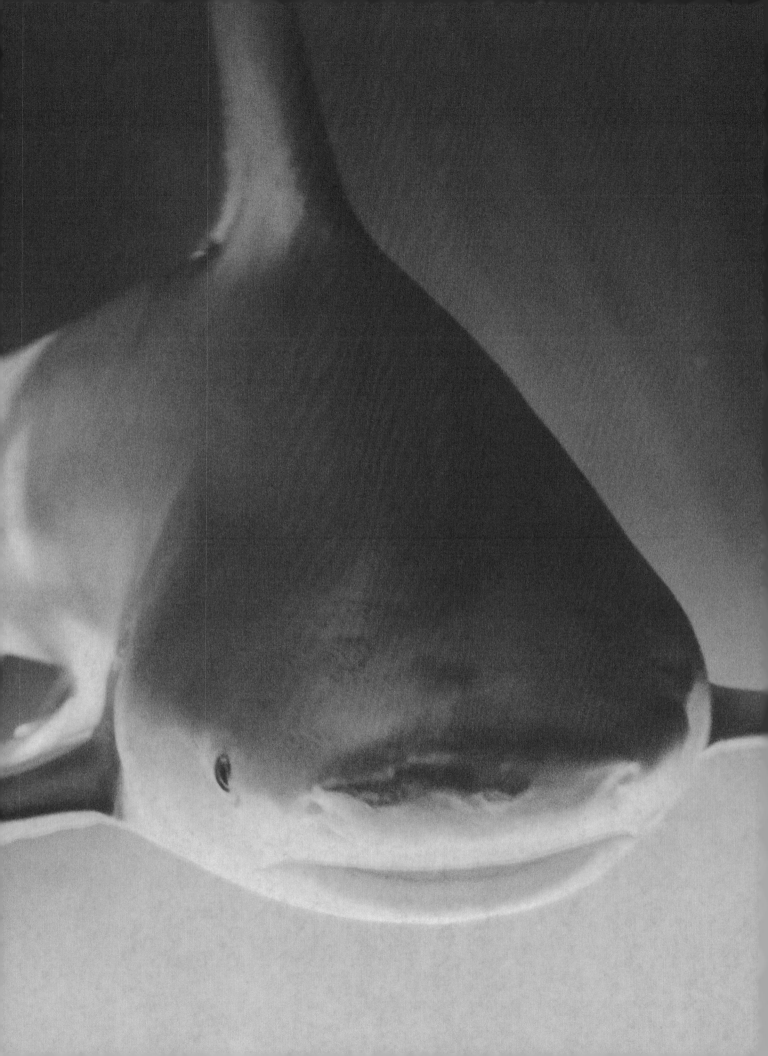

Many people believe that sharks only live in the oceans. However, they are distributed in bodies of water found all over the world.

There are more than 300 different species of sharks in the ocean but they all share the same basic anatomy. Anatomic shark characteristics have made them ruthless predators.

Sharks engage in different forms of communication. Although sharks are loners, they have the intelligence to communicate.

Sharks have been on Earth for almost 450 million years, although modern sharks have evolved for 100 million years.

The Dermal denticles that covers Shark skin is so tough and hard that before the invention of sandpaper, shark skin was used to polish wood.

You are 1,000 times more likely to drown in the sea than you are to be bitten by a shark.

Sharks rarely pose a danger to humans. But humans do pose a danger to sharks! Fishermen kill an estimated 30 million to 100 million sharks every year. About 75 shark species are in danger of becoming extinct.

Sharks don't chew their food; they rip off chunks of meat and swallow them whole. They can last a month or two without another big meal.

CPSIA information can be obtained at www.ICGtesting.com
Printed in the USA
LVOW02s1054110215

426617LV00011B/158/P